Transformative Judaism: Sacrificial Cult to Righteousness

Arthur Finkle

Transformative Judaism: Sacrificial Cult to Righteousness

Hadassa Word Press

Publisher:
Hadassa Word Press
is a trademark of
International Book Market Service Ltd., member of OmniScriptum Publishing Group
17 Meldrum Street, Beau Bassin 71504, Mauritius

Printed at: see last page
ISBN: 978-3-639-79462-5

Transformative Judaism: Sacrificial Cult to Righteousness

Arthur L. Finkle

Contents

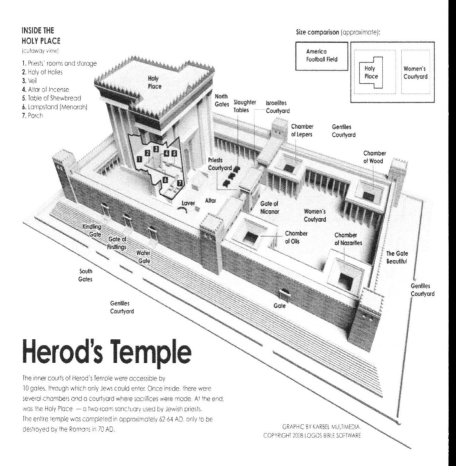

INSIDE THE HOLY PLACE
(cutaway view)

1. Priests' rooms and storage
2. Holy of Holies
3. Veil
4. Altar of Incense
5. Table of Shewbread
6. Lampstand (Menorah)
7. Porch

Size comparison (approximate):

America Football Field

Holy Place

Women's Courtyard

Holy Place

North Gates

Slaughter Tables

Israelites Courtyard

Chamber of Lepers

Gentiles Courtyard

Chamber of Wood

Priests Courtyard

Laver

Altar

Gate of Nicanor

Women's Courtyard

Kindling Gate

Gate of Firstlings

Water Gate

South Gates

Chamber of Oils

Chamber of Nazarites

The Gate Beautiful

Gentiles Courtyard

Gentiles Courtyard

Gate

Herod's Temple

The inner courts of Herod's Temple were accessible by
10 gates, through which only Jews could enter. Once inside, there were
several chambers and a courtyard where sacrifices were made. At the end,
was the Holy Place — a two-room sanctuary used by Jewish priests.
The entire temple was completed in approximately 62-64 AD, only to be
destroyed by the Romans in 70 AD.

GRAPHIC BY KARBEL MULTIMEDIA.
COPYRIGHT 2008 LOGOS BIBLE SOFTWARE

Figure 1 Holy Temple

Dedication and Acknowledgements

This work is dedicated to Linda, my understanding wife of more than 50 years. I also owed a debt of gratitude to my Rabbi Jack Pianko, z'l as well as my editor at Hadassa Word Press, Evghenia Tulbure.

Preface

This penning brings to life an overlooked subject in contemporary Judaism – how did the ancient Jewish tradition, rooted in the Temple rituals transform itself after the Destruction of the Second Temple.

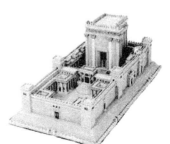

Figure 2 Second Temple

As you will find, this transformation did not occur immediately nor did the Rabbi's automatically accede to leadership.

Indeed, competing sects of the Israelite religion vied for a leadership role. To understand, I have described the internecine fighting; the compromises of transforming the Jewish rites by including symbols of the Holy Temple; and its syncretization through the years.

For one thousand years, the Israelites (Jews) worshipped in a Holy Space at the Temple in Jerusalem. Before the construction of the Temple ()there were two), the Holy of Holies, which contained the Law revealed to Moses and a small amount of manna), became the dwelling place for the Shechina (God's presence). Indeed, there was a cloud hovering over the holy of holies for the 40-year journey through the dessert and the years leading up to the construction of the First Temple.

In Exodus 25–31 and 35–40, the scribes cited this tabernacle (Hebrew: מִשְׁכָּן, mishkan, meaning "residence") as the dwelling place of God).

More importantly, the Babylonian Talmud is replete with Temple ritual and rites, reminding scholars of the importance of the continuity of tradition in transformation of a culture from one phase of history to another.

Today's Jews be they Orthodox or Liberal often fail to take notice of this significant transformation of a vital civilization under the weight of mercurial history.

There was an inner sanctuary, the Holy of Holies, created by the veil suspended by four pillars., containing the Ark of the Covenant (where the Laws resided).

On the south side stood a table, on which lay the shewbread. On the north side was the Menorah, holding seven oil lamps to give light. On the west side, just before the veil, was the golden altar of incense.

After about 200 years, the Israelites decided to build a Temple to house the Holy of Holies, with God's imprecation:

> *Speak to the children of Israel, that they bring me an offering: of every man that gives it willingly with his heart ye shall take my offering. And this was the offering which you shall take of them; gold and silver and brass... (Exodus 25, 2-3).*

Thus, the priority of holiness began with precious metals (Menorah and Cherubim (gold), Lavar (brass), Silver (Bowls) and brass (bowls).

Sacred Space

> The Eternal One spoke to Moses, saying:
> Tell the Israelite people to bring Me gifts;
> you shall accept gifts for Me from every
> person whose heart is so moved. . ... And
> let them make Me a sanctuary that I may
> dwell among them" (Exodus 25:1-8). And
> eleven chapters later we read, " 'The
> people are bringing more than is needed
> for the tasks entailed in the work that the
> Eternal has commanded to be done.'
> Moses thereupon had this proclamation
> made throughout the camp: 'Let no man
> or woman make further effort toward gifts
> for the sanctuary! So, the people stopped
> bringing: their efforts had been more than
> enough for all the tasks to be done" (36:5-
> 7).

Two themes were central to this Torah portion: Building
the Mikdash (the Holy Space), ultimately understood as the
Temple in Jerusalem that housed God's presence; Contributions
to build and decorate this Temple come from people whose
hearts had been so moved to give, voluntarily.

Their main mission was to gather the exiles and rebuild the
Temple (Ezra 5:15). God not only commanded the construction
of a physical Sanctuary of stones or wood; God desired the whole
Earth to be His Resting Place. He wants each person to be a
Sanctuary for His Divine Presence.

Therefore, the Blessed Holy One will give three gifts (Wisdom,
Understanding and Knowledge) by which the Sanctuary was

made) to all Israel. (Noted is the custom in the Diaspora of using dirt from Israel, preferably Jerusalem, in the burial coffin of the diseased.) [1]

In Kabbalah, the Midrash makes a mystical connection between sacred space and the immanence of the Shechinah (Hebrew word meaning "dwelling" denotes the dwelling or settling of the divine presence).

After the destruction of the Second Temple, the Jewish rite fluctuated from one group of believers to another.

The Eternal Holiness of Jerusalem

The Talmud proclaimed Jerusalem as eternally holy, even if most Jews lived in the Diaspora. (Makkot 19a 19b)

The Gemara cited a case where Rabbi Yishmael ruled that the law of separating sacrificial Second Fruits existed. No longer eaten in Jerusalem, the law separating the tithe, applied during the post-Temple period because the Gemara (Babylonian Talmud) assumed that the holiness of the Land of Israel remained eternal.

The Rambam (14th century Spanish commentator), distinguished between Jerusalem's holiness and the antiquated practice of tithing.

With Jews returned to Israel under Ezra, the Scribe, the seat of the Almighty derived its holiness from Jerusalem. Rambam ruled that the destruction of the Temple did not eliminate Jerusalem's eternal holiness.

Building the Second Temple

> "I have called by Name Betzalel son of Uri… and I have filled him with the spirit of God, with Wisdom, with Understanding and with Knowledge" (Ex 31:3).

In Hebrew, Betzalel meant "In the shadow of the Mighty one". Accordingly, Betzalel walked the steps of God.

What did he do to be in the Shadow of God? He dwelled in the secret place of the Highest, as in the verse: "He that dwells in the secret place of the Highest shall abide in the Shadow (Betzel) of Shaddai" (Ps. 91:1).

Betzalel reflected God's Light; he resembled God; and since God's purpose with Creation was to create a "Permanent Home for his Divine Presence", He chose Betzalel to build the Holy Sanctuary. Accordingly, God attributed the three Upper Attributes of Creation (the Three Upper Sefirot – called: Habad).

- Hokhma (wisdom) – "By Wisdom HaShem founded the Earth."
- Binah (understanding) – "By understanding he established heavens."
- Daat (knowledge) – "By his knowledge the depths were broken, and the sky drop down the dew." (Prov 3:19-20).[2]

The Rabbi's incorporated the idea of sacred spaced to universalize the Diaspora in synagogues, homes and Jewish institutions.

Betzalel created the Second Temple as if he were creating the world, in the image of God. The "Image of God" (Tzelem Elokim) in Gematria equals the Phrase: "I will resemble the Highest" (Adameh leElion) (Is 14:14). [3]

Tabernacle

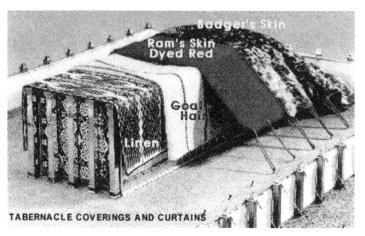

Figure 3 Tabernacle

From Moses' exodus from Egypt to the construction of the First Temple in Jerusalem on 1000 BCE (approximately 200 years), the Holy of Holies sited in the portable Tabernacle.

Figure 4 Holy of Holies surrounded by Cherubim (Angels),

Remembrance of Destroyed Temple

Priests added salt to sacrifices. Breaking bread denoted the shewbread stand of twelve loafs. The seven-branched menorah in the Temple reflected Jewish themes in synagogue Temple and burial designs. [4]

Figure 5 Table of Shewbread

In addition, The Rabbi's expressed remembrance of the Temple's destruction in customs, such as intentionally leaving incomplete a part of a dwelling; omitting a bauble in formal dress and the smashing of the glass at the end of the Marriage ceremony. [5]

Figure 6 Traditional Breaking the glass at a wedding in remembrance of the Temple's Destruction

Figure 7 Laver of Copper

Eternal Light (Ner Tamid)

The Rabbi's decreed that an Eternal Light (Ner Tamid) hang above the ark in every synagogue. This eternal light symbolized the menorah, the seven-branched lamp stand which stood in front of the Temple in Jerusalem, always lit. [6]

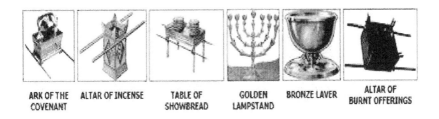

ARK OF THE COVENANT   ALTAR OF INCENSE   TABLE OF SHOWBREAD   GOLDEN LAMPSTAND   BRONZE LAVER   ALTAR OF BURNT OFFERINGS

Figure 8 Temple Implements

Several Jewish Movements – Post Destruction

Samaritans

Early disagreements on pagan worship

Trouble started not long after Moses brought the twelve tribes of Israel to the Promised Land. At the death of Solomon in 975 B.C., the kingdom of Israel was split into two parts, Judah in the south, and Samaria in the north. The two kingdoms were often in disagreement. The northern kings loved their pagan idols and were constantly at odds with Jerusalem.

Conquering armies

When the Assyrians conquered Acre (where Samarians lived) in 724 B.C., the inhabitants of Judah were not sympathetic.

The emergence of the Samaritans as an ethnic and religious community distinct from other Levant peoples appears to have occurred at some point after the Assyrian conquest of the Israelites when the Assyrians exchanged populations with the Israelites in the Sumerian Kingdom of Israel in approximately 721 BCE. The records of Sargon II of Assyria indicated the deportation of 27,290 inhabitants of the former kingdom.

Jewish tradition affirms population replacement but suggested a different ethnic origin for the Samaritans. The Talmud accounts for a people called "Cuthim" on a number of occasions, mentioning their arrival by the hands of the Assyrians. According to the Bible and Josephus, Sargon II, King of the Assyrians moved the population of Israelite population of Samaria to Halah to Gozanon along the Khabur River and to the towns of the Medes in Assyria. Replacing them, The king of the Assyrians brought Babylonian peoples from Babylon, Cuthah, Avah, Emath, and Sepharvaim. [7]

Assyria fell to the Egyptians a hundred years later. Egypt conquered the Assyrians. Then, Babylon (the successor state to Assyria) defeated the Egyptians. In 586 B.C., the Southern Kingdom of Israel fell to the Babylonians. The literati and the richer Jews exiled to Babylon. They adapted well, founding major Religious Academies.

Post-exilic Disagreements

When the Babylonians allowed the Judeans to return to their homeland, the rift between the Samaritans (many of mixed pagan-Samaritan couplings) and the Judeans widened.

Some sources indicated that the builders of the Second Temple refused Samaritan assistance because of their pagan impurity. Other sources say the Samaritans refused to help their brothers of Judah to rebuild.

According to Samaritan tradition, the split between them and the Judean-led Southern Israelites began during the biblical time of the priest Eli, when the Southern Israelites split off from the Northern and Central Israelite tradition. [8]

In the Talmud, a post-exilic religious text of Rabbinic Judaism, the Rabbi's cited the Samaritans as Cutheans, referring to the ancient city of Kutha, geographically located in what is today Iraq. [9]

In the biblical account, however, Kuthah was one of several cities from which people were brought to Samaria to worship Nergal, a pagan god.[10]

Nergal was, in part a solar deity, sometimes identified with Shamash, representative of a certain phase of the sun. Portrayed in hymns and myths as a god of war and pestilence, Nergal represented the sun of noontime and of the summer solstice both of which bring destruction. [11]

Samaritanism, closely related to Judaism, believed that their worship, based on the Samaritan Pentateuch, was the true religion of the ancient Israelites before the Babylonian captivity. The Samaritan claimed they preserved the religion's customs and ceremonies, remaining in the Land of Israel. Different from the adulterated Judaism of those returning from the Babylonian Captivity, the Samaritans believed that Mount Gerizim was the original Holy Place of Israel from the time that Joshua conquered Canaan. The location of sacred space (The Temple Mount of Moriah in Jerusalem; or Mount Gerizim became the major issue between Jews and Samaritans). [12]

Moreover, returning Jews from Babylon began rebuilding their temple. While the Prophet, Nehemiah, built the walls of Jerusalem, the Samaritans vigorously attempted to halt the undertaking (Nehemiah 6:1-14).

Thereupon, the Samaritans built a temple for themselves on Mount Gerizim, which the Samaritans insisted that Moses designated as a sacred place of worship.

Sanballat, the leader of the Samaritans, established his son-in-law, Manasses, as high priest, continuing the schism.

In addition, Samaria became a refuge for outlaws of Judea (Joshua 20:6-7; 21:21). The Samaritans willingly received Jewish criminals.

The violators of the Jewish laws, and those who had been excommunicated, found safety for themselves in Samaria, greatly increasing the hatred which existed between the two nations.

Moreover, the Samaritans adhered strictly to the five books of Moses. They rejected the writings, the prophets and subsequent Jewish traditions.

In biblical times, Samaritans numbers more than one million. Today there are fewer the one thousand. [13]

Pharisee Movement

The Pharisee movement probably began when Ezra and Nehemiah (5th cent. BCE) reinstituted Torah-based Judaism in Judah (Southern kinddom). Ezra read the Torah to the People. The Men of the Great Assembly interpreted the Oral Law and developed a body of laws, customs and traditions.

Josephus, a Jewish historian stated that the Pharisees opposed the Sadducees in 169 BCE. The Pharisees held that God gave two Torahs to the Jewish People on Mount Sinai: the written (Torah, codified into 39 books after the Temple's destruction) and the Oral Torah (interpretations and emandations of Torah law. Centuries later, The Rabbi's confirmed t his dating in the Mishna, Talmud, Responsa, Bereitot, etc.). The movement democratized the Jewish religion, arguing that the worship of One God was not confined to the Temple of Jerusalem. Instead it fostered prayer to replace the sacrificial cult, fostered synagogue worship and home expression of Jewish laws.

The Pharisees provided the elasticity and continuity of the Jewish tradition by applying the Torah to contemporary problems.

The Pharisees did not recognize hierarchical divisions of Jewish practitioners. No longer did Priests and Levites have the privileged role as religious functionaries.

The Pharisees represented the lay community. The Rabbi's constructed a life framework for the masses through the Midrash (ethical parables and folktales) and the Mishnah (codification of all laws found in the Bible).

The Pharisees appeared in sharp contrast to the Sadducees, who represented heirs, lineage to their aristocratic functionaries.

John Hyrcanus, a Hasmonean leader indicated there existed completely different shape and form of the Pharisees compared to other groups.

After the Romans assumed power (63 BCE), the Pharisees reverted to their original role as teachers of Jewish law and arbitrators of the community's internal disputes. This did not mean that they abdicated their right to speak out and act on the political issues of the day, as is evidenced by the pro-revolt stand taken by R. Simeon ben Gamaliel I and other Pharisee leaders in the early days of the revolt against the Romans (66-73 CE) and also during the Bar Kokhba revolt of 132-135 CE.

The Pharisee world (unlike the Sadducees) produced Jewish scholars graduating from Academies of religious learning. Great schools of Hillel and Shammai were already flourishing in the first century BCE, in the in the Upper Galilee.

Yavnah boasted a bet midrash (house of learning), known as Kerem Be-Yavneh, before the destruction of the Temple in 70 CE. The town with its academy assumed a central role when the Pharisaic sage, R. Jochanan Ben Zakkai, The Pharisees became more significance under the leadership of R. Jochanan's successor, R. Gamaliel II. The Pharisee-oriented academy created basic and far-reaching decisions in Jewish law and practice. Some of these decisions involved the retention of the Jewish Calendar; codifying daily Amidah prayer; accepting the legal rulings of the School of Hillel as against those of the School of Shammai (competing schools of thought). The New Testament representation of the Pharisees polemicized seemingly stringent Jewish law. However, the Nazarenes (early Christians were fighting a religio-polito-philosophical war with the Pharisees.)

Talmudic literature showed the simplicity of the sages' ways, their concern for their fellow Jews, belief in freedom of choice, respect for elders and their general involvement in the totality of Jewish society.

Josephus noted: "Because of these views they are ... extremely influential among the townsfolk," and that the "great tribute" paid by the Jewish population to "the excellence" of the Pharisees lies in their practice of the highest ideals. [14]

The Talmud recorded several differences between the Sadducees and the Pharisees. These include the dating of the Shavuot festival; the validity of certain ordained ceremonies on Sukkot (the festive Water Drawing ceremony, among others); and the punishment of false witnesses. They also differed on matters of belief, with the Sadducees, rejecting the belief in an Afterlife, the resurrection, and the Messiah, all basic to the Pharisees.

The Pharisees recreated sacred space. They substituted the Synagogue for the Temple. The Synagogue's uses were threefold: prayer, assembly and study.

The sages developed various strategies of representing different types of Jews. They settled on the term, "Israel" for themselves. Those who did not live by their values and laws were considered ignorant (the so-called 'ammei ha'arez) or the Samaritans (kutim) or the sectarian (e.g., minim and Sadducees).

At the same time, they believed that the rules by which they lived were the patrimony of all Jews, even if the Jews themselves rejected that patrimony. To that end, they presented themselves as the continuers of ancient tradition, rather than as innovative sectarians. Secondly, as self-conscious "traditionalists," they could not accept certain interpretations of Torah law.

Sadducee Movement

The Sadducees were one of main Jewish political and religious movements in the years between 150 BCE and 70 CE. (The other movements were the Essenes and the Pharisees.) They had a conservative outlook and accepted only the written Law of Moses. Many wealthy Jews were Sadducees or sympathized with them.

No Sadducee texts were known; their ideas and opinions were only known from hostile sources. The Pharisees were vehemently opposed to the Sadducees and consequently, the few passages in the rabbinical literature that refer to the Sadducees negatively portray them. For example, when Pharisee teachers were discussing whether a good person could become an evil person, the example of a Pharisee who went over to the Sadducees was quoted as proof that people could become evil.

Another text stated that the Sadducee sect started as a group of Pharisee heretics. Several other sources were not kind to the Sadducees. The Jewish historian, Flavius Josephus, recorded that the behavior of the Sadducees towards others was smug. And their behaviors with one another were savage.

The Christian texts portray the Sadducees as opponents of Jesus of Nazareth:

> 'Take heed and beware of the leaven of the Pharisees and the Sadducees. (Matthew 16.1-6).

The above passage appeared in the Gospel of Mark, where only the Pharisees are mentioned: the author of the gospel of Matthew added the Sadducees.

Without direct sources, we cannot give a systematic account of the ideas of the Sadducees. Nonetheless, indirect sources mention several aspects of Sadducee theology.

The fundamental difference between the Sadducees and the Pharisees was the interpretation of the Law of Moses (i.e., the five first books of the Bible, the Torah). The Sadducees maintained that the only way for truly pious behavior was to live according to the commandments in the Written Law; the Pharisees, on the other hand, taught that God gave both the Written and Oral Laws to the Jews. Therefore, Jews could interpret the Written Law. After all, the world had changed since the days of Moses. Consequently, the Pharisees said that the 'Written Torah' was to be supplemented with 'the Oral Torah', the interpretation of the written Law by the Pharisee teachers, the rabbis. The Sadducees considered this an almost blasphemous act, because it seemed to deny the majesty of the original Law of Moses.

The fact that the Sadducees focused on the five first books of the Bible did not mean that they denied the Prophets and the Writings, that completed the Hebrew Scriptures. But they refused to accept the other Biblical books as sources of law. When a Sadducee judged a case, he ignored the oral Torah, stressing the importance of the Temple Priests. In contrast, the Pharisees insisted on the up-to-date interpretation of the law.

In practice, the Law of Moses is not always very clear, and the Sadducees had interpretative traditions of their own, which were written down in a book of jurisprudence known as the Book of Decrees. This penal code, known from a rabbinical source, the Megilla Ta'anit, stated that the Book of Decrees was revoked on the fourth of Tammuz (no year is given). The code was very harsh: the author of the Megilla Ta'anit stated that the Sadducees had taken the famous line Exodus 21.24, 'an eye for an eye', literally. While the Sadducees would blind the transgressor's eye, the Pharisees allowed the transgressed to pay damages.

Sadducee theology posited that souls die with the bodies. Pharisees believed in the resurrection of the souls. The rabbinical text known as 'Avot de Rabbi Nathan' stated that a discussion about this subject was the cause of the schism between Pharisees and Sadducees.

Subsequently, the Sadducees and the Boethusians split into two sects,

Boethusians

A Jewish sect closely related to the Sadducees. The Boethusians adhered to Antigonus' of Soko Midrash: "Be not like the servants who serve their masters for the sake of the wages but be rather like those who serve without thought of receiving wages."

Two students, Zadok and Boethus, popularized this ethic. Consequently, the Boethusians (and Sadducees) rejected an afterlife and a resurrection.

The Boethusians lived in luxury because they wanted to live a full life on Earth because they did not believe in the afterlife. [15] Accordingly, their theology was materialistic and non-transcendent.

A Midrash (moral stories based on Jewish Law) claimed both the sects represented the rich. The Mishnah (codification of the Torah into Jewish Law), as well as Baraitot (caselaw that did not enter the Mishna) cited that the Boethusians opposed the Pharisees' law that the omer be counted on the second day of Passover. Pentecost, seven weeks and one day later, should always be celebrated on Sunday. The

Boethusians also conspired with false witnesses with the intention of misleading the Pharisees in the determination of the new moon. [16]

There is little known about this sect. The Talmud mentioned a Boethusian in a dispute with a pupil of Rabbi Akiva; yet it is probable that the word here means simply a sectarian or a heretic, just as the Rabbi's used the term "Sadducee" in a much wider sense. [17]

The Boethusians were the "High Priests" mentioned by Josephus, as opposed to the lower Priests, which comprised the Sadducee and Essene party. They were installed into the Priesthood by Herod in a politically astute move; Herod was very fearful of the High Priesthood and the power held by that position. (Herod was tyrannical. He murdered many Hasmoneans, including his own wife and children.), He deliberately imported the Alexandrian branch of the Priesthood, that had left Jerusalem prior to the Hasmonean rebellion against Antiochus. They left because they were allied with the Egyptian, Hellenist party and were enemies of the Hasmoneans. [18]

Although the historical value of this anecdote is questionable, it may be noted that the date of the schism (two generations after Antigonus, i.e., 140 BCE) neatly fits the probable date of origin of the Sadducee movement. Whatever its reliability, the story cited the refusal to believe in the resurrection.

The Pharisees and Christians, on the other hand, believed in the resurrection of the dead. When the Christian teacher Paul explained his ideas to a court of Pharisees and Sadducees, he found it easy to create division among his judges.

In the New Testament, when Paul perceived that one part were Sadducees and the other Pharisees, he cried out in the council, 'Men and brethren, I am a Pharisee, the son of a Pharisee; concerning the hope and resurrection of the dead I am being judged!' (Acts 23:6)

After Paul made this statement, dissension arose between the Pharisees and the Sadducees. Sadducees believed there was no resurrection, nor angels nor spirits; but the Pharisees confess both. The Pharisaical scribes protested, finding no evil. If a spirit or an angel has spoken to him, do not resist God.

However, the author of Acts exaggerated a bit. No Sadducee denied that messengers of God (Mal'ach Adonay) were mentioned in the five first books of the Bible. However, many other Jews started to believe that these messengers were winged celestial beings, although no scriptural evidence existed.

The historian Flavius Josephus stated that the Sadducees did not believe in Fate.

Pharisees claimed people possessed free will. Essenes affirmed that Fate governed all things. Sadducees claimed that fate did not exist.

Flavius Josephus gave a summary of Pharisee and Sadducee thought. He posited that the Pharisees were most skillful in the exact interpretation of Jewish law. Josephus claimed that the Pharisees ascribed to Fate and God, allowing for the power of humankind. All souls were incorruptible. But souls of good humans were removed into other bodies and that the souls of bad men were subject to eternal punishment.

The Sadducees were a conservative group. They never adapted the Aramaic script or to normative thought.

The high Priesthood descended from the Zadokite family. Therefore, the Sadducee movement originated in opposition against the Hasmonaean revolt against Seleucid Greeks.

Whatever their relation to the Hasmonaeans, the Sadducees remained deeply involved in the Temple cult in Jerusalem for more than two centuries. The kings supported the Sadducees, who had great influence on royal policy. Only under the reign of Queen Alexandra Salome (76-67 BCE), did the Pharisee leader, Prince Simeon ben Shetah, overcome the Sadducees in the high court (Sanhedrin). But even during these years, the Sadducees retained some power. In the confused years after the death of the Queen, they regained much of their former influence.

When Herod, the Great became sole ruler of Judea in 40 CE, he appointed High Priests of his own choosing. The Sadducees remained involved in the management of the Temple, as was the case during the Roman occupation (6-70 CE), when the Roman governors appointed the High Priest, they chose among the Sadducee families.

The Jewish elite sympathized with the ideas of the Sadducees. The Pharisees (common people) maintained a more egalitarian worldview.

After the destruction of Jerusalem and its Temple in 70 CE., the Priests had no function because their duties concerned the Temple that had ceased to exist[19]

The Essenes

Until the discovery of the Dead Sea Scrolls in the Judean wilderness, the only material available on the Essenes came from the classical historians. Because the community was semi-monastic and separatist, it was not surprising that information was incomplete.

Figure 9 Dead Sea Scrolls

Philo of Alexandria (c. 20 B.C.--50 A.D.) cited the Essene Sect. He idealized the Essenes to allow fellow Greeks to understand this small movement. [20]

There are three major accounts of the Essenes in Josephus' writings. The best-known works (shortly after 70 CE) are Josephus' *History of the Jewish Wars* and *Jewish Antiquities.* Josephus compared the Essenes to Pythagoras, the Pharisees to the Stoics and the Sadducees to the Epicureans. [21]

The elder Pliny, a Latin writer who accompanied Titus in the Jerusalem war, briefly mentioned the Essenes. [22]

The Dead Sea scrolls did not specifically mention the Sadducees, but used the code name, 'Manasse.' In a commentary on the prophet

Nahum, we read that, when the end of times occurred, the rule of Manasse would terminate (women, babies and little children will be imprisoned, and will be put to death by the sword).

The Essenes, probably the Qumran Sect, separated from the other Jews. They partook in common meals; required admission to the sect; interpreted Jewish Law; and believed in predestination [23]

Where does 'Essene' emanate?

The Greek name *Essenoi* is related to the Aramaic *hasya*, "pious." Moreover, Philo in a couple of places connects the name with Greek hosiotas, "piety" or "holiness."[24] Thus, the name is an Aramaic plural of the Semitic word for "pious." The Hebrew equivalent would be hasidim, "the pious" or faithful. This usage of the verb shows that the word was not limited to Eastern Aramaic. [25]

James Strong cited the Essene as founder communal living group.[26] No one could blaspheme him. He was the Teacher of Righteousness. [27]

Pliny cited an Essene community on the shore of the Dead Sea, just north of Engada and Masada. But other Essenes lived in towns and villages and had an open house policy for traveling. [28]

In the different orders of the sect, Josephus referred to its characteristic admission, requiring a postulant to live outside the camp for a year with minimal provisions and follow the rules of discipline. If the putative entrant remained faithful, he could draw near to the purification water. Then, after two more years as a novitiate, he could take the oath and join the meal. [29]

The Essenes were ascetics. Their life was one of self-denial for the performance of virtuous acts. They had no money, no luxuries, no pleasures of love (with women); they sought contentment AWAY from the world.

The Essenes held all things in common. They were indeed a brotherhood; all activity was for the common good of the community. When they joined, they relinquished all their personal property? When they worked, their salaries were handed over to a common purse.

If any were in need, they could simply take from the common supplies. No one had a private house, although communal for the dwellings were open to all travelers. [30]

Any Essene traveling could therefore go unencumbered, except for being armed for safety.

The Essene orders differed on marriage and children. Most Essenes were celibate, except for adopted children for instruction.

Regarding marriage, Philo claimed that the Essenes banned marriage because women were selfish, jealous, deceitful, seducing. Indeed, they avoided spiritual enrichment because they the cared for children. [31]

Josephus. living with the Essenes for three years, remarked that marriage was important to continue the sect; therefore, some Essenes married only for the purpose of procreation. [32]

Essenes' ideals included perfuming virtuous deeds for which they could achieve immortality of the soul. They also feared eternal punishment.
33

They vowed piety to God, justice to humankind, hatred of the wicked and love for the just. They also promised to love those in the sect, love truth, conceal nothing from one another and reveal nothing to outsiders.

Diligent workers, the Essenes fled the unholy cities but still worked in their occupations-, but only for the common good.

In their daily routine, they arose in silence (no speaking until after the ancestral prayer facing the sun). Thereafter, they tended to their crafts, working late into the afternoon.

Then, they reassembled, bathed in cold water, entered a sacred room. A Priest prayed, then the community ate; prayed again; ending with Priest's blessing of God. They returned to their work. Thereupon, they dined. To an outsider their silence remained a mystery. [34]

Strictly observant, they also functioned as scribes and prophets, studying and preserving the Scriptures, the books of their sect, and the names of angels.

They worshipped in obedience to the Law. They participated in daily instruction. During instruction, they sat in order, one man reading; another elder explaining.

They disagreed over the sacrificial cult, either because of the Priesthood or the calendar (they followed the solar calendar of Jubilees). They sent offerings to the Temple, but no sacrifices; they made the sacrifices in their own territory. Strictly ritually purified, they washed in cold water. [35]

The Essenes maintained strict discipline; sinners were expelled from the camp, often dying of starvation. The community took many of them back at their last gasp, believing that they had suffered for the expiation of their sins

Some of their laws were very detailed. For example, one could not spit on the Sabbath. The Essenes rigorously observed the Sabbath day. [36]

But they cared for their needy, the sick, the elderly, travelers, and anyone else in need with provisions provided for out of a communal purse. As a result, many of them lived to a ripe old age of 100. [37]

Valuing life's virtues and hoping the glorious world to come, they endured Roman persecution because they prioritized a glorious death over capitulation.

The Essenes believed that the body was corruptible. Only death could free the soul in order to enter the heavenly world. [38]

Nazarenes

The "sect of the Nazarenes" appeared in the Book of Acts (New Testament). Paul was accused of being a ringleader of the sect of the Nazarenes. (Acts 24:5). [39]

Abraham Geiger, German Jewish theologian and a product of the Enlightenment, depicted Jesus as a Pharisee, following Jewish Law. On the other hand, Geiger identified Paul as the actual founder of normative Christianity. Paul's theology, the gospel of John, and subsequent Church pronouncement deviate from Judaism by adopting Pagan beliefs and rites. [40]

Fourth-century Nazarenes were originally Jewish converts of the Apostles, who fled Jerusalem because of Jesus' prophecy of its coming siege (during the Great Jewish Revolt in 70 AD). They fled to Pella, northeast of Jerusalem of what is now Jordan. [41]

The Nazarenes initially considered themselves Jews; maintained an adherence to the Law of Moses; and used only the Aramaic Gospel of the Hebrews, rejecting all the Canonical gospels and the concept of Jesus being the Son of God.

The term simply designated followers Jesus the Nazarene. Later, in the first to fourth centuries, the term changed from followers of Jesus to Christians. [42]

As late as the eleventh century, Cardinal Humbert, Benedictine Abbot in France referred to the Nazarene sect as Sabbath-keeping Christians.

Modern scholars suggested the Nazarene sect existed well into the eleventh century. Gregorius of Bergamo, in 1250 CE, wrote concerning the Nazarenes as the Pasagians. These Pasagians lived in Lombardy in the late 12th or early 13th century.

Gregorius claimed these Pasagians retained the Old Testament rules and laws of Moses (circumcision, kosher foods, and the Jewish holy days). [43]

The Rabbi's Retained Reminders of the Holy Temple

When the Jerusalem Temple ceased to function (70 CE), the functionless priesthood catalyzed The Rabbi's to redefine sacrifice. Covenant and atonement, long defining Israelite religion, did not disappear. In their place, the Rabbi's substituted the performance of certain activities as "sacrifice" by other means. Fasting and repentance, prayer and study, good deeds (charity and hospitality) became surrogates for adhering to the Covenant and for atonement of sins.

The Rabbi's devised a variety of strategies (asceticization, domestication, spiritualization, and textualization) bespeaking self-sacrifice, in which action became the surrogate for the sacrifice.

Such revisions continued into the Middle Ages, considering the tabernacle and Temple to be miniature models of the entire universe. [44]

They carefully utilized the ideas of Sacred Space and universalized the ethical Code of Jewish Law in lieu of the Sacrificial Cult.

Hebrew Calendar

The Rabbi's propounded the same calendar, modified in 386 CE by Hillel II, to account for the verbal equinox.

The times of Sacrifices became the times for religious services. On Rosh Hashanah, the Shofar sounded as it did in the Temple.

The ark represented the Holy of Holies. It contained perochet (curtains); the Torah dressed as the Kohen Gadol; the Torah's Choshen .(breast plate represented the Twelve Hebrew Tribes) replaced the High Priest's amulet; and the Keter (crown worn by the High Priest) crowned the Torah.

The Torah appeared in scroll form through the ages. Special Sabbaths modeled those in the Temple:

Shabbat Shuvah (Return) referred to the ten days of repentance that fell in between Rosh Hashana and Yom Kippur.

Shabbat Shirah (Song) was a special Shabbat that includes in the Torah reading of Shirat ha-Yam (The Song at the Sea; Exod. 15:1-18). The Israelites sang this Song of the Sea after crossing the Red Sea in safety. It also commemorated the destruction of the pursuing Egyptian army during the crossing. And the song registered hope for the future.

The tax year began on Shabbat Shkalim. The Year of the Trees began of Tu B'shvat 15 Shvat (full moon); the last new year, Elul, is the New Year for the tithing of cattle (Elul 29-30).

The Rabbi's decided to orient the Ark toward Jerusalem (the East in the Western Hemisphere), in commemoration of the sacred space of Jerusalem. [45]

The new Jewish community honored three pilgrimage festivals (Pesach, Shavuot and Sukkot. Agricultural in origin (the autumnal harvest, the harvest of the barley; the harvest of the wheat).

Passover

Figure 10 Seder Plate

Pesach fell on 15th of Nissan, when a full moon appears. The ancients counted months by new moons. A full moon, the middle of the month, usually signified something significant. Jewish Law requires the eating of Matza to remember our servitude and subsequent freedom in the Promised Land (Israel).

The Passover ceremony in the Temple included pouring sacrificial lambs' blood into golden and silver bowls. The Mishnah stated:

> *The Torah required that the sacrifice be offered publicly. On the 14 day of Nisan, the Kohanim (Priests) would open the doors of the Temple and allow the people to offer sacrifices in three large groups of no less than thirty people.* [46]

A Choir of Levites sang. When the process began, the Shofar sounded with the three traditional sounds: tekiah; teruah; tekiah and the choir recited the Hallel prayer. This music continued until the groups made both the Pesach offering and an additional sacrifice, (Hagiga offering).

Origin of Hallel (Included on Special Days)

The Hallel (a prayer consisting of Psalms 113 through 118) sanctified the pilgrimage festivals . Traditional Jews recites the Hallel as praise and thanksgiving on Passover, Shavuot and Sukkot (and some other occasions, such a Hanukkah and the New Moons, known as Rosh Chodesh).

Figure 11 Passover - Spring Holiday

During the Passover in the Temple, there was a ceremony with golden and silver bowls through which the sacrificial blood of lambs was Pesach, the Priests sounded the shofar was sounded 3-times each for three parts of the Temple ceremony. The Mishnah stated:

> The Torah required that the sacrifice be offered publicly. On the 14 day of Nisan the Kohanim (Priests) would open the doors of the Temple and allow the people to offer sacrifices in three large groups of no less than thirty people but each group which usually were more numerous than the minimum.
>
> Behind the Kohanim on a platform stood the Choir of Levites. When the process began, the Shofar sounded with the three traditional sounds: tekiah; teruah; tekiah and the choir recited the Hallel prayer.

This music continued until the entire group offered both the Pesach offering and an additional sacrifice, called the Hagiga offering. (The first meat eaten was the meat of the Hagiga sacrifice and then later the Passover Sacrifice which was eaten with bitter herbs and matzah.) [47]

The Jewish Spiritual Leaders recited he Hallel prayers (Psalms 113 through 118) to spiritualize the three pilgrimage festivals. Recited by observant Jews to give gratitude for Jewish holidays, including Passover, Shavuot and Sukkot and on other occasions such as Hanukkah and the New Moon (Rosh Chodesh).

Feast of Weeks (Shavuot)

"You shall bring your first fruits to the House of the Lord your God... " (Ex. 23:19.)

Figure 12 Giving the LAW

Jewish Pentecost falls 50-days after the second day of Passover. This Feast of Weeks memorialized Moses' receiving the Ten Commandments (written and oral laws) on Mount Sinai during the 40-years of wondering the dessert.

Shavuot originally commemorated the harvest of the Spring barley and the planting of the wheat. The Rabbi's spiritualized it to remember the Revelation of the Law at Mount Sinai.

Shavuot literally means "weeks;" Shavuot is thus known as the Festival of Weeks. It is called so because it culminates the seven-week period of the counting the omer (day) which begins on the second day of Passover, when the omer barley offering was brought to the Temple and the wheat was planted. But the Bible also refers to it as the "Feast of First Fruits" (Exodus 23:16, Numbers 28:26), and the First Fruits cannot be brought to the Temple until then.

Figure 13 Feast of Weeks, Harvest of Wheat

In many ways this festival was the celebration of the agricultural yield of Israel itself. The bringing of the First Fruits to the Holy Temple manifested the land's intrinsic holiness. Mandated by a Biblical commandment, the Shavuot offering of "First Fruits" were the first fruits of the season.

This Divine commandment did not include every species of fruit, but only those of the "seven species for which the Land of Israel was praised," as described by the verse in Deut. 8:8: wheat, barley, grapes, figs, pomegranates, olives, dates and honey.

> For the LORD your God is bringing you into a good land...a land of wheat and barley, of vines and fig trees and pomegranates, a land of olive trees and honey. (Deuteronomy 8:7-8)

The Priest shall take the basket place it before the altar of the Lord your G-d. You shall then make the following declaration before the Lord your G-d:

> My ancestor was a homeless Aramaean. He went down to Egypt and sojourned there with a small number of men, but there he became a great, mighty, and populous nation. The Egyptians were cruel to us and caused us to suffer; they placed harsh slavery upon us. We cried out to the Lord, the G-d of our fathers, and He heard our voice and saw our suffering, our harsh labor, and our distress. (Deuteronomy 26:5.)

Jewish Prayer Yearning to Return to Zion

To commemorate the Temple's destruction and the yearning to return, Jewish prayer invoked the return to Zion.

Zion and Jerusalem are mentioned five times in Amidah prayer (central prayer of Jewish liturgy). It called for the restoration of Jerusalem. The Rabbi's ordained that all synagogues be in the direction of Jerusalem.

In the additional service for festival, holidays and the Sabbath, the Musaf prayer states:

"But because of our sins we have been exiled from our land and sent far from our soil...Draw our scattered ones near among the nations and bring in our dispersions from the ends of the earth. Bring us to Zion your city in glad song, and to Jerusalem home of your sanctuary in eternal joy."

As part of the Jewish Torah Service (the Sabbath, Mondays, Thursdays, New Months, and major Jewish Holidays), the congregation sings: "For out of Zion shall go forth the Torah, and the word of the Lord from."

In the Meal Grace After Meals Jerusalem is mentioned: *"Have mercy Lord, our God...on Jerusalem Your city, on Zion the resting place of Your glory..."* and "Rebuild Jerusalem, the holy city, soon in our days. Blessed are you God who rebuilds Jerusalem in His mercy."

The thanksgiving blessing after a light meal stated:

> Have mercy, Lord, our God...on Jerusalem, Your city; and on Zion, the resting place of Your glory... Rebuild Jerusalem, the city of holiness, speedily in our days. Bring us up into it and gladden us in its rebuilding and let us eat from its fruit and be satisfied with its goodness and bless You upon it in holiness and purity. [48]

On Tisha B'Av (day commemorating destruction of the First and Second temples, among other catastrophes that occurred on that day, a prayer petitioned God to comfort those who mourn the destruction of Zion and Jerusalem. The prayer began with, "Comfort, Lord our God, the mourners of Zion and the mourners of Jerusalem."

It concluded with "Blessed art Thou, Lord, who brings comfort to Zion and rebuilds Jerusalem."

*In a Sabbath eve prayer: "Blessed are You Lord, who spreads the shelter of peace over us, over His entire people Israel, and over Jerusalem." [49]

The conclusion of the Passover Seder, the participants proclaimed:

> The Passover Seder is now completed in accordance
> with its laws, all its ordinances and statutes. Just as
> we merited to perform it, so may we merit to offer it.
> O Pure One, Who dwells on high, uplift the
> congregation (Israel) who cannot be counted. Soon,
> and with rejoicing, lead the offshoots of the stock that
> You have planted, redeemed, to Zion. Next year in
> Jerusalem! [50]

This prayer not only denoted a geographical space that housed sacred space but bespeaks the hopes and aspirations of becoming the Holy Nation that God promised the Jews. [51]

Shavuot came seven weeks after the second day of Passover. Originally celebrating the wheat harvest, The Rabbi's attributed the religious of the anniversary when God gave the Torah to the nation of Israel assembled at Mount Sinai. It also honored the Yahrzeit (anniversary of the death) of King David. The Chasidim commemorate the Yarzeit of the Ball Shem Tov, founder of Hasidism.

The religious days remained the same. Rosh Hashanah initiated the new religious year on the first of Tishrei (September-October). Ten days later, Yom Kippur served a personal and communal confessional and remission of sins.

Sukkot

Figure 14 Sukkot

Sukkot occurred as the harvest festival in gratitude for agricultural abundance. Falling on the 14th Tishrei (full moon). Sukkot, a Hebrew word meaning "booths" or "huts," referred to the Jewish festival of giving thanks for the fall harvest. [52]

The Rabbi's redefined the holiday with the religious meaning of the freed slaves dwelling in temporary shelters during the 40-yuears of trekking the dessert from Egypt to Israel.

Water Libation Ceremony

On Sukkot, the Priest officiated at The Water Libation Ceremony that prayed for precious rains, essential to a good crop yield. (Succah Bavli 37; and RH 16a).

Another interpretation from the Midrash is that the lower waters were sad when God separated the waters to upper and lower. Their distress was noted by God that the lower waters would be elevated during this season. (Rabbaynu Bachya to Lev 1:13.)

The Water Libation ceremony was an elaborate ritual emitting great joy, in fulfilling of Isaiah 12:3-4: 'You shall draw water with joy from the wellsprings of salvation.

Transition of Water Willow Dance to Hoshana Rabbah

The name for this holiday probably comes from Psalm 118:25. Hoshana means to save. This is the seventh day of the Feast of Tabernacles. It comes one day before Shemini Atzeret. It is usually observed on the 21st day of the Hebrew month Tishrei. It is also called "the great Hosanna."

Figure 15 Hoshana Rabbah

This practice in the Temple served the basis for our modern custom of Hosannas. As reported by The TUR (14th century German-Spanish Legalist, in Orech Chaim (a compendium of laws), congregants circled the bema (platform for prayer leaders) once a day with a Torah being taken to the serving as the focal point and in place of the altar. Participants carried a Torah to emulate Temple times in which the marchers recited the name of God while walking. According to the Palestinian Talmud), such a practice reflected not only what had transpired during the time of the Temple, but also staged a reenactment of the siege and conquering of Jericho in the time of Joshua, when the conquerors circled the city once a day for six days and seven times on the final day, causing the walls to come tumbling down (Joshua 6).

R. Joseph Caro (compiler of the Code of Jewish Law, 1565) noted that, on Hoshana Rabbah (seventh day of Sukkot), even a person who did not possess the four species (palm branch, myrtle, water willow and etrog) participated in seven laps around the bimah, carrying the Torah. Caro thus created a special remembrance of a Temple ritual.

Rav Moshe Feinstein (mid-20th century) noted a custom to recite the Hosannahs after Additional Service, like the extra sacrifice offered in the Temple on special festival days.[53]

Rabbinic Jewish Period of Talmud Development

Ancient Judaism focused on the sacred space of the Tabernacle in the Temple. To give homage to God through the means of the day – sacrifice, both animal and grain. However, Rabbinical Judaism did not focus on sacrifices. Rather, they accentuated Torah-observance. In ancient times, the sacrifices were mitzvas (obligations). When the Temple no longer existed, the Rabbi's substituted prayer, compassion and ethics as obligations.

Without a location of sacred space, Rabbinic Judaism became more universal rather than particular to the land of Israel. Rabbinical debates continue to this day as to whether Rabbinical Judaism is universal to all or only to Jews.

When the Temple was destroyed for a second time, many in Israel desired to abstain from the consumption of meat and wine. R. Joshua replied tauntingly, "My sons, why do you refrain from eating meat and drinking wine?' They replied, "Shall we eat meat that was once offered on the altar but is no longer? Shall we drink wine that used to be poured in libations upon the altar, but is no longer?" [R. Joshua] replied to them, "If so, let us desist from eating bread, for we no longer offer Minchah offerings [whose primary component was loaves of bread]. And should you suggest that we eat only fruit, why, fruit we should desist from as well, for we can no longer bring the first fruits. And should you suggest that we eat other types of fruit [that are exempt from the laws of the first fruits], then [consider that] we should desist from drinking water as well, for the libations of water upon the altar have desisted! . . . My sons, come and let me tell you. To abstain from mourning is impossible, for this evil decree [that is, the destruction of the Temple] has indeed befallen us. Yet we cannot mourn excessively either, for we do not enact a decree that the people cannot tolerate.... Rather, the sages have said, let a man build a house and leave a portion unfinished, and so forth."

Indeed, Tractate Sanhedrin warns against excessive mourning the loss of the Temple so as not to dwell in the past and to choose life to continue living lives.

The Rabbi's re-interpreted Jewish Law. Customs varied regionally. Living inside or outside Israel affected some rituals.

Traditional Judaism most closely resembled ancient Rabbinic Judaism to the extent of practicing Jewish law (halacha). Liberal Judaism has a more flexible approach but retained Judaism's core values.

Traditional Judaism most closely resembles ancient Judaism to their degree of practicing religious law (halacha). Liberal Judaism has a more flexible approach, but their source is still the full Bible.

Torah Principles Remained Virtually the Same.

Judaism possessed no creed. There were Torah principles that the Rabbi's retained, such as Monotheism (Belief on One God who demanded righteousness).

Jewish laws governed Orthodox Jewry

Some rites changed:

1) The Rabbi's canonized the Tanakh with agreement by a special Sanhedrin (Rabbinical court). (Berakhot 33a.).

2) Purim and Hanukkah became post-biblical festivals.

3) Certain fasts commemorated the Destruction of the Temple.

4) Sacrifices ceased.

5) The Rabbi's devised a calendar. No longer was it necessary to testify as to the New Moon. (Rabbi Hillel II, 360 CE.)

6) The oral law (Mishna and Talmud) became written when the official writings became too hard to memorize.

7) Saying the blessings over food (and on various occasions).

8) Washing one's hands before eating bread.

9) Lighting the Hanukkah-menorah.

10) The Eruv (earmarking the acceptable distances one can walk during the Sabbath and some Festivals.

11) Reciting the Hallel prayer (Psalms (113–118), on festivals.

12) Requirement to Light Sabbath candles.

13) Reading the Book of Esther on Purim.

Figure 16 Seven-Branched Menorah

Roman General (then Emperor) Vespasian gave Yochanan ben Zakkai permission to set up an Academy at Yavneh (Yavne was one of the major ancient cities in the southern coastal plain, situated 12.5 miles south of Jaffa).

Roman rule was mercurial from until 193-211 CC, when Roman Emperor, Lucious Septimus Severus treated Jews relatively well, allowing them to hold public office and be exempt from Roman rules that interfered with religious practices.

Rabbi Akiva became a lightning rod in consolidating Rabbinic Judaism. In 200 CE, the Rabbi's codified the Mishnah (Jewish oral law) compiled/edited from all the Torah law.

Figure 17 Mishnah

In 203 CE, due to health, Judah HaNasi relocated the center of Jewish learning from Beth Shearim to Sepphoris (Galilee). In 212 CE, Roman Emperor Caracalla allowed free Jews to become full Roman citizens.

In 220 CE, superior Babylonian academies existed in Babylonia (Sura and Pampadita)

Figure 18 Talmud Page

In 380 CE, the Rabbi's completed the Jerusalem Talmud. In approximately 450 CE, the Rabbi's completed the more authoritative Babylonian Talmud. The learned Rabbi's considered the arguments and scholarship the Babylonian Talmud superior to the Jerusalem Talmud.

The Talmud is a commentary on the Mishnah. Subsequently, the Savoraim, Geonim, Rishomim and Acharonim in commented on this commentary, such that Jewish law became dynamic.). See Below

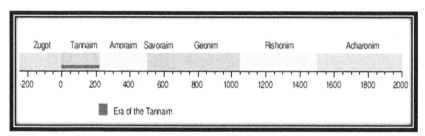

Jewish   Time - Continuation of Temple Practices

Rituals followed the rites of the Temple calendar: Weekdays, the Sabbath, the three Pilgrimage festivals (Sukkot, Pesach and Shavuot).

The Rabbi's decreed three services a day, identical to the times of the Temple sacrifices.

An interesting custom arose from Rabbi Moshe Sofer (known as the Chatam Sofer). He claimed that, while Jewish law did not require all graves to face any particular direction, a custom arose that bodies were buried with feet facing the entrance to the cemetery, to symbolize that they will leave the cemetery at the time of the resurrection of the dead.

At the time of the resurrection, everyone will head to the Land of Israel. Accordingly, some cemeteries were constructed so that the feet of the corpse faced the direction to travel to Israel.[54]

The New Moons

The Rabbi's continued the lunar calendar with correction for solar year. 55 Beginning with a Babylonian influence, the Rabbi's used a LUNAR calendar from 10-220 BCE.

The Talmudic Rabbi's (200–500 CE) used mathematical rules to correct for the solar year for an agricultural ec0onoimy.

Maimonides' work replaced counting the years since the destruction of the Temple substituting the norm of modern creation-era Anno Mundi.

The Hebrew lunar year is about eleven days shorter than the solar year and uses the 19-year Metonic cycle to bring it into line with the solar year, with the addition of an intercalary month every two or three years, for a total of seven times per 19 years.[56]

Figure 19 Moon Phases

Convergence of Torah Adornment and Temple's High Priest

The Golden Garments (8th) of the Kohen Gadol Shemot 28:4:42

Gold plate plate worn on the Kohen Gadol's forhead :

קדש ליהוה

Holiness unto YHVH
Atone for arrogance atitude

Mitre (turban)
Fine linen
Atone for pride of his countenance (Psa 10:4)

2 onyx stones, each stone has grave 6 names of tribe of Israel vs 9-10

Sardius, topz, Carbuncle

The Breastplate of Judgement (Choshen) which 12 precious stones vs 17-21

Emerald; Sapphire; Diamond

Ligure, Agate; Amethyst

Hidden in the Breastplate of Judgement contain the Urim and the Thummim (to determine YHVH's will) vs 30

Beryl; Onyx; Jasper

bind the breastplate by the rings

Girdle (a sash) is type of believer always ready, waiting, humility in character & willing to serve. Yeshua display John 13:4-10 the washing Talmidim's feet and in Rev 1:13 we see Him in Golden girdle Atone for Sinful heart

with a lace of blue, may be above the curious girdle of the ephod, and that the breastplate be not loosed from the ephod

Ephod: - embroidered with blue, purple scarlet and gold (heavenly glory) vs 6
Atone for idolary

The incense of Fragrance full enjoyment of His glory. YHVH's copyright

Robe of the Ephod
Atone for evil speech
Colossians 3:8
Techelet

golden Bell & Promegranates of blue, purple & scarlet vs 33-34 when the priest walk the bell sound in the Holy Place if it does not sound we know he die vs 35 when the bell sound he was alive

Fine Linen Tunic
Atone for killing

The pants inner clothes atones for sexual Trangression Matthew 5:28

Walk in bare foot standing Holy Ground

Figure 20 Garments of High Priest

Figure 21 Adorned Torah

As previosly mentioned, the Torah adronments represented the holiness, similar to those of the High Priest in mistake.

Both were adorned with crowns amd textile vestments. The Choshen (breastplate representing the 12-tribes) adorned both. The Torah cover pictures thwe 10-commndments that housed in the Holy of Holies.

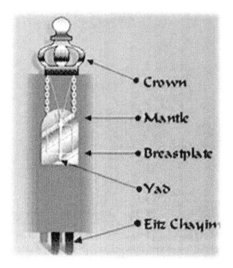

Figure 22 Torah Decorations

Retention of the Two Religious Holidays

Rosh Hashanah

In Leviticus, we read:

> *In the seventh month on the first day of the month, you shall observe complete rest, a sacred occasion commemorated with loud blasts. You shall not work at your occupations; and you shall bring an offering by fire to the Lord (Leviticus 23:24-25).*

In Numbers, we read:

> In the seventh month, on the first day of the month, you shall observe a sacred occasion: you shall not work at your occupations.... You shall observe it as a day when the horn is

sounded. You shall present a burnt offering of pleasing odor to the Lord (Numbers 29:1-2).

Figure 23 Rosh Hashana

The sacred number 'seven' is critical. Just as the seventh day of the week is holy, so the seventh month of the year has special significance. This special sacredness is commemorated by the sounding of the shofar, the ram's horn.

Aside from sacrifice, this is the only specific action mandated for this day in the Torah. Sounding the shofar is mentioned in both sets of verses, although no explanation or reason is offered. Taken together, the three elements of these verses--the lack of a name for the holiday, of a reason for the celebration, and of an explanation for sounding the shofar --pose a puzzle for us: why doesn't the Torah describe or emphasize this holy day any further?

When the seventh month arrived, the entire people assembled in the square before the Temple Water Gate. Traditionally begun by Ezra, the scribe, a Scribe read from the scroll of the Teaching of Moses. (Nehemiah 8:1-3).

The People of Israel renewed their covenant with God. Some wept when they realized how far they had sinned.

But they were admonished not to mourn because "this day is holy to the Lord your God" (Nehemiah 8:9).

The Rabbi's valued special importance for the beginning of the Religious Year. Indeed, it bespoke the new religious year and the penitential season:

> "The Lord looks down from heaven, He sees all mankind. From His dwelling place. He gazes on all the inhabitants of the earth, He who fashions the hearts of them all, who discerns all their doings" (Psalms 33:13-15) (Mishnah Rosh Hashanah 1.2). [57]

The Scriptures indicated that "the blast of the horn" (tekiat shofar) sounded on the first day of the seventh month (Rosh Hashanah), as an exceptional rite. Nevertheless, there were numerous verses that cite hatzotzerot (trumpets) associated the sacrificial cult, performed by King Hezekiah. Hatzotzerot indeed played a significant role. Yet the Bible generally associated "blasts of sound" with the Shofar, announcing assembly, travel or war. [58]

Apparently hatzotzerot were the usual Temple musical instruments whereas Shofar was only for special occasions. [59]

The Mishanic, Tractate *Rosh Hashanah* associated the Shofar after destruction of Temple, (RH. 137f.; the Shofar, announcing Messiah, (San. 654); the Shofar and the Bet Din (RH. 137ff.); the Shofar blessings over, (RH. 120); children; its physical composition offerings; the kosher shofar; order of the blasts; practicing; and other Shofar matters.

Compromise on the Shofar Notes

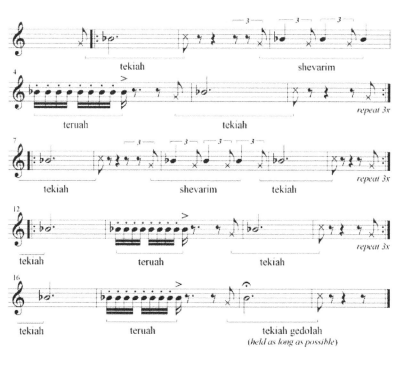

We did, however, know that the Sages discussed the configuration of the notes as they were played in the Temple. They knew what the tekiah note was (a blast). However, these Sages whose fathers had probably heard the Shofar soundings in the Temple, could not remember the correct playing of the teruah (whether it was three sobbing sounds or nine staccato sounds). Accordingly, to accommodate both schools, they compromised by inventing the shevarim and played both the teruah and shevarim to be certain the sound was correct. [60]

Unlike the first day of the seventh month [which became known as Rosh Hashanah], the 10th day has a specific designation and purpose in the Torah, with elaborate rites connected to it:

> Mark, the 10th day of the seventh month is the Day of Atonement. It shall be a sacred occasion for you; you shall practice self-denial, and you shall bring an offering by fire to the Lord; and you shall do no work throughout that day. For it is a Day of Atonement, on which expiation is made on your behalf before the Lord your God... Do no work whatever; it is a law for all time, throughout the generations in all your settlements. It shall be a Sabbath of complete rest for you, and you shall practice self-denial; on the ninth day of the month at evening, from evening to evening, you shall observe this your Sabbath. (Lev. 23:27-32).

The designation of this day was reiterated in Numbers:

> On the 10th of the same seventh month you shall observe a
> sacred occasion when you shall practice self-denial. You shall do
> no work. (Num. 29:7).

Self-denial--inui nefesh in Hebrew (literally, afflicting one's soul) --
traditionally has been understood to refer to fasting. For the Israelites,
this Day of Atonement was therefore a day for fasting and complete
cessation of work, observed by individuals in their homes and
settlements.

While observed today as a time for individual atonement, the biblical
Yom Kippur is primarily a Priestly institution:

> "The Priest who has been anointed and ordained to serve as
> Priest in place of his father shall make expiation. He shall put on
> the linen vestments, the sacral vestments. He shall purge the
> inmost Shrine; he shall purge the Tent of Meeting and the altar;
> and he shall make expiation for the Priests and for all the people
> of the congregation " (Lev. 16:29-33).

Yom Kippur

The High Priest performed Yom Kippur rituals in the holy of holies where God's presence existed.

The High Priest's presence became so important that he was given a red string from which to pull him out of the Holy of Holies should he die. He also maintained a conditional divorce to his wife, should he die.

And there was a High Priest in waiting, should the High Priest succumb so as not to perform the sacred Yom Kippur ritual to expiate the sins of the community of Israel. [61]

Five times, the High Priest changed his clothes after ritual purification of holy water in the ritual bath (mikveh).

A literal scapegoat (pushed from a cliff to his death) commemorated the symbolic communal expiation of sins for the community of Israel as represented by a goat (Scapegoat). There were two young goats. One was sacrificed by the High Priest, while the other was sent to his death over a cliff and attested to by Temple.

The Priest brought a sin offering that would "make expiation for himself and his household" (Lev. 16:11), to enter the Holy of Holies and place sacrificial blood on the cover of the ark, known as the "atonement seat" (Lev. 16:12-14), and thus to "make expiation in the Shrine" (Lev. 16:17).
62

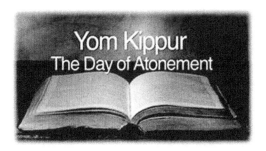

Figure 24 Yom Kippur - Day of Atonement

On Yom Kippur, the Shofar heralded the Jubilee Year once, every fifty years [Lev.25:8]). The Bible proclaimed theat Jubilee Year provided for no agricultural work; all slaves went free; and all land returned to its original owners (or heirs).

The Rabbi's reconfigured this solemn holiday by requiring fasting and mandating special prayers of penitence.

Prayers for Return to Jerusalem

The creators of prayer books, from 200 CE, repeatedly referenced the future return to Jerusalem. See Appendix A., p. 84.

Role of the Shofar

The Palestinian Talmud (Sukkot 31b) portrayed the important role of the shofar in the Holy Temple during this holiday.

Nine shofar blasts heralded the additional sacrifice (Musaf), (commemorating New Moons, festivals, and other special days.

Prior to the Sabbath, on Friday, the shofar sounded 6-blasts. The first three blasts for cessation of labor to prepare for the Sabbath. The latter three sounds to separate the sacred from the profane in order to officially begin the Sabbath.

Figure 25 Sounding Shofars and Trumpets

Fast Days Commemorated Temple Period

Fast Days Commemorated Temple Period. Jewish Fast days (the absence of food and drink for 24 hours. fasting demonstrated contrition of sin that darkened the history of the Jewish People. Except for the Fast of Esther, all are Biblical.

Shulchan Aruch

The Shulchan Aruch (the Code of Jewish Law) served to codify halacha (Jewish law). Authored by Rabbi Yosef Karo in the 16th century. Together with its commentaries, it was generally considered the most widely accepted and authoritative compilation of halacha.

The halachic rulings in the Shulchan Aruch generally follow Sephardic (Spanish Jewish) law and customs. Moshe Isserlis (Rema), an Ashkenazic Jew, glossed the Shulchan Aruch, noting where the Sephardic and Ashkenazic customs differ. These glosses were called the mappah ("tablecloth") to the Shulchan Aruch's ("Setting the Table"). Accordingly, , the Shulchan Aruch, came to reflect Rav Karo's work as well as Rav Isserlis',

With its commentaries, The Code of Jewish Law was the baseline in Jewish Law, it grew through Maimonides' Mishneh Torah, the Talmud commentaries, themselves, and authoritative commentaries covering 1600 years. The Chafetz Chaim updated the section concerning Jewish worship practices in 1900.

Fasts Commemorating Biblical Events

The only Chumash-based (Pentateuch) fast was The Day of Atonement, Yom Kippur (Lev. 16:29–31; 23:27–32; Num. 29:7ff.).

The Ninth of Av (Tishah b'Av), commemorated the day of mourning for the destruction of the First and Second Temples (see Jer. 52:12–13 where, however, the date is given as the Tenth), and other calamitous occasions.

The 17th of Tammuz, remembered the breaching of the walls of Jerusalem in the First Temple period (Jer. 39:2 where the date is the 9th) and Titus' breaching the walls of Jerusalem, and of other calamities which befell the Jewish people (Babylonian Talmud, Ta'an. 4:6, Ta'an. 28b. Shulchan Aruch, OH, 549:2.

The Tenth of Tevet, in memory of the siege of Jerusalem by Nebuchadnezzar , king of Babylon (II Kings 25:1–2, Jer. 52:4ff.; Ezek. 24:1–2).

The Third of Tishri, called Tsum Gedalyah (the Fast of Gedaliah), in memory of the slaying of Gedaliah (Jewish Governor appointed by the Babylonians after Babylonian hegemony. (Jer. 41:1–2; II Kings 25:25).

The Fast of Esther (Ta'anit Ester) on the 13th of Adar, the day before Purim (Esth. 4:16).

Besides the Day of Atonement, the other four fast days were observed in the period of the Second Temple. Zechariah prophesied that they would be transformed into days of joy and gladness (Zech. 8:19).

On the Day of Atonement and on the Ninth of Av, fasting is observed by total abstention from food and drink from sunset until nightfall of the following day; on the other fast days, the fasts were less stringent. Pregnant and nursing women involving the health of the fetus and/or mother certain circumstances were exempt from observance (Sh. Ar., OḤ, 50:1 (Isserles) and 554:5).

Fasts Decreed by The Rabbis

During the Ten Days of Penitence (i.e., between Rosh Ha-Shanah and the Day of Atonement) and as many days as possible during the month of Elul (Sh. Ar., OH, 581:2).

The first Monday and Thursday, and the following Monday after Passover and Sukkot (Tur and Sh. Ar., OH, 492). This fast atoned for possible sins committed in excessive celebration during the holidays (Tos. to Kid. 81a S.V. Sekava).

During the Three Weeks of Mourning between the 17th of Tammuz and the Ninth of Av (Tur. and Sh. Ar., OH, 551:16).

The Seventh of Adar, traditional date of the death of Moses observed in many communities by the members of the hevrah kaddishah ("burial society").

Yom Kippur Katan ("Minor Yom Kippur"), the last day of each month, on which many communities fasted and recited a special liturgy.

The eve of Passover, firstborn males' fast as a symbol of the sanctification of the Jewish firstborn who were saved during the tenth plague in Egypt (Ex. 13:1ff.).

Days commemorating disastrous events in Jewish history (full list in Tur and Sh. Ar., OH, 580:2).

Private Fasts

The anniversary (yahrzeit) of a parent's death or of that of a teacher (Ned. 12a).

The groom and the bride fast on their wedding day until the ceremony (Isserles to Sh. Ar., EH, 61:1), unless it is Rosh Ḥodesh (Isserles to Sh. Ar., OḤ, 573:1).

To avert the evil consequences of nightmares (Ta'anit Ḥalom). In Talmudic times because The Rabbi's believed that bad dreams could have pernicious effects (Shab. 11a). In later centuries, however, the obligatory nature of this fast was mitigated by halakhic authorities (see Sh. Ar., OḤ, 288, 5).

If a Torah scroll were dropped, those present fasted a day. [63]

Symbolic Retention of the Kohanim (Priests)

The Temple's destruction catalyzed Judaism to redefine sacrifice. The Rabbi's repackaged the core covenant and atonement principles by redefining sacrifice. They revised meaning contained prayer fasting, good deeds, charity, hospitality and the following Jewish law. [64]

Symbolic Retention of the Kohanim (Priests)

The Temple's destruction catalyzed Judaism to redefine sacrifice. Like surrounding practices of the sacrificial cult, the Rabbi's repackaged the core covenant and atonement principles by redefining sacrifice. The revise meaning contained prayer fasting, good deeds, charity, hospitality and the following Jewish law.

The Rabbi's redefined them after the destruction for at least three or four generations, for example, taking the times for sacrifices into the times for thrice daily prayer, recited for over 20 centuries by religious Jews. In addition., the Rabbi's created prayers:

To gather exiles from the four corners of the earth

To restore a judicial system, with judicial authority granted to Jewish judges to apply Jewish law and justice.

To defeat enemies who seek to destroy the Jewish culture.

To demonstrate that righteousness is the Jewish ideal.

To return to Jerusalem, to dwell in it, to build the Temple and to reestablish the Davidic dynasty.

To restore the Temple to the service to God.

To redeem Israel.

To give peace to Israel[65]

Shaye Cohen claimed that that the synagogue provided a democratization of the priestly functions., In a utopian spirt, Cohen proclaimed that the Restoration movement will lead to the Messianic Era, enable all Jews, not just the male hereditary Priests, to participate in the rites and rituals of the Jewish culture. [66]

There is evidence that synagogues sprouted up during the Babylonian Captivity and returned to Israel when the Diaspora completed in 550 CE. Nonetheless, until the year 70 C.E., the Jewish worship focal point was Jerusalem temple, where a hereditary priesthood offered sacrifices as described in the Hebrew Bible.

Synagogue worship was not a biblical requirement; thus, many first-century Jews probably did not consider it necessary.

However, without the Temple, synagogues provided already-established communal institutions that would ultimately develop into the new centers of Jewish worship, learning and assembly. [67]

Because the Torah-based Jewish Priesthood held a traditional role in Jewish tradition (direct descendants of Aaron, the original Kohen).

The line of the Kohanim was patrilineal, passed from father to son without interruption from Aaron, for 3,300 years (more than 100 generations.

Interestingly, Dr. Karl Skorecki, a Sephardi medical researcher at the University of Toronto and the Rambam-Technion Medical Center in Haifa, involved himself in the breakthroughs in molecular genetics (DNA).

He found is his studies, that Kohanim are descendants of one man (Aaron). They had a common set of genetic markers--a common haplotype.

An analysis of the Y chromosome markers of the Kohanim and non-Kohanim were significant. The marker, (YAP-) recurred in 98.5 percent of the Kohanim (and a significantly lower percentage on non-Kohanim).

A Blessing Forever

Just as the Kohanim's lineage spanned more than 3,000 years, The Rabbi's gave this group duties (honors) in the synagogue(). They applied the Priestly blessing. They received the first Aliyah for reading the Torah. They are also forbidden in certain funeral practices.

Sephardic custom, as written in the Shulchan Aruch, is for the Kohanim to bless the congregation every day, The Ashkenazi custom became an occurrence on holidays. In Israel, following the commentary of the Vilna Gaon (1720 – 1797), the Rabbi's restored the practice to recite the blessing every day and twice on Shabbat, Rosh Chodesh and Yom Tov. [68]

Synagogue

The institution of the synagogue began with the return of the exiles from Babylon in IN 519 BCE. In some instances, it replaced the academies in Babylon. In other instances, it became a center of learning and prayer.

Return of the Exiles

The return of the exiles in Babylon radically charged the Jewish culture.

In the second century BCE and onwards, with documentary evidence, different were leadership models, political institutions, literary genres, and religious ideas.

Institutions such as the Gerousia (Peoples' Courts, a Greek invention), religious doctrines such as resurrection and the Oral Law (at least as far as the Pharisees are concerned), ritual practices (i.e., the miqweh-ritual bath), burial customs, sectarian organizational forms, the genre of apocalypse, the institution of conversion, and more all crystallized during these centuries. Another important development currently was the emergence of the ancient synagogue

Initially, the synagogue served an Assembly Hall and study center, probably after the Babylonian exile (537 BCE). After the fall of Babylon to the Persian king Cyrus the Great in 537 BC, exiled Jews began to return to the land of Judah. King Cyrus the Great ended the exile of the Jewish people in 537 BC, the year after he conquered Babylonia, granting permission to return to Israel and rebuild the Temple (Second

Temple 521-516 BC) under Zerubbabel Its origins as a place of worship[probably occurred after the destruction of the Second Temple (70 CE) (Ezra chapters 1-6- return; Ezra chapters 7-10)-Nehemiah became political ruler.

Sacred Space

The synagogue served as Sacred Space for worship, education, and communal affairs has a murky history. One tradition dated it to the Babylonian exile return in the 6th cent. B.C.E.

The returnees may have brought back with them the basic structure that became the synagogue, developed by the 1st cent. CE. Such a changeover was incremental. The basilica probably served for religious rites, legal courts and assemblies.

After the Destructions of the Temple, this school defined the synagogue that housed Jewish religious, intellectual, and communal life.

Other scholars hold that the synagogue arose after the Hasmonean revolt (167–164 BCE) as a Pharisaic alternative to the Temple cult. The destruction of the Temple (A.D. 70) and the Diaspora over the following centuries increased the synagogue's importance.

Magdala Excavations

Magdala, first settled during the Hasmonean rule, created a wave of settlement activity in Galilee. Settlers probably came from Judea. It flourished in the Early Roman period, as documented by the New Testament and Josephus.

The fertile geographic area of northern Sea of Galilee attracted farmers.

During the Great Revolt, precedent to the Temple's Destruction, Josephus mentioned the place in the list of the Galilean fortified strongholds.

The dig in the town itself yielded paved streets, a marketplace, system of urban drainages, and residential quarters with several water installations identified as a unique type of Jewish ritual baths (miqwa'ot). .

Fig. 4. Magdala's synagogue, 1stcentury CE, looking West. Photograph by the Magdala Center, 2009. Courtesy Marcela Zapata-Meza.

The importance of Magdala's synagogue was its dating. It was a Frist century synagogue during the Great Revolt. To put it another way, this synagogue and the Temple existed at the same time. . A synagogue contemporaneous to the Temple is still a rare finding. Rachel Hachlili lists nine sites identified beyond doubt as synagogues from the Second Temple period. The preservation of some is very partial. Also, some of these structures operated only for a very short period, not more than a few years, such as the rebel's synagogue on Masada. [69]

Synagogue Services were simpler and more democratic than those in the Temple, where only the hereditary Priesthood presided. [70]

Documentary testimony to the synagogue is replete in the New Testament, process of writing between

The earliest such texts are the letters (or Epistles) written between about 50 and 62 AD by St Paul to various early Christian communities.

Acts of the Apostles, a description of the missionary efforts of Peter and others in Jerusalem and of Paul on his journeys. 70-90.

This account is believed to be the work of Luke, who probably writes it between about AD 75 and 90.

The earliest version to survive in the Bible is Mark's Gospel. It was probably written between AD 75 and 85,

In the middle of the 2nd century it becomes evident that a great many different and often contradictory passages of holy scripture are circulating among the various Christian churches, each claiming to offer the truth. (There is even a Gospel according to Judas Iscariot.) Which of these shall be accepted as the official canon? This becomes a subject of urgent debate among church leaders.

By the end of the century it is widely agreed that four Gospels, the Epistles of Paul and the Acts of the Apostles are authentic. But it is not until 367 that a list is circulated by Athanasius, bishop of Alexandria, which finally establishes the content of the New Testament. [71]

According to Gospels, Jesus often taught in synagogues, (Mark 1:21-28), in northern Israel. The book of Acts suggests that the apostle Paul also taught in synagogues (Acts 17:1-2).

"Synagogue, by the first century C.E. they were found in both Palestine and the Diaspora, where they were used for a variety of communal needs: as schools (Josephus, Antiquities 16.43), for communal meals (Josephus, Antiquities 14.214-216), as hostels, as courts (Acts 22:19), as a place to collect and distribute charity (Matt 6:2), and for political meetings (Josephus, Life 276-289). Worship also took place in first-century synagogues, although this would not develop into something like modern Jewish synagogue worship until much later.

Nonetheless, reading and interpreting the Torah and Prophets is well attested in first-century synagogues (Acts 15:21), and although scholars disagree about the extent of communal prayers, literary sources suggest that Jews prayed in at least some synagogues at this time (Matt 6:5; Josephus, Life 280-295).

Rabbinic leadership of synagogues (which is what we are familiar with today) was limited in the first few centuries C.E. and didn't crystallize until the medieval period.

Although the structure in Capernaum (Israel) dated several centuries after the Temple's Destruction, evidence for a first-century synagogue is disputed. Nonetheless, there are remains of a few first-century synagogues in Israel and Palestine, including buildings in Gamla, Masada, and Herodium. [72]

Though synagogues were found in some first-century communities, their status as places of worship were limited and restricted as to events.

After the temple was destroyed in 70 C.E. Without the temple, synagogues provided already-established communal institutions that would ultimately develop into the new centers of Jewish worship. [73]

In the Tosephta, Rabbi. Judah declared

> "Whoever has never seen the double colonnade [the basilica-synagogue] of Alexandria in Egypt has never seen Israel's glory in his entire life. It was a kind of large basilica, one colonnade inside another.,. with a wooden platform in the middle. The minister of the synagogue stood on it, with flags in his hand. When one began to read, the other would have the flags, and they would answer 'Amen'. . . . They did not sit in a jumble, but the goldsmiths sat by themselves, the silver smiths by themselves, the weavers (0"Z11f) by themselves, the bronze workers (0"01t) by themselves,4 and the blacksmiths by themselves. All this for what? So that when a traveler came along, he could find his fellow craftsmen, and on that basis, he could earn a living."

In the Tosefta in many ways, the Tosefta acts as a supplement to the Mishnah (tosefta means "supplement, addition"). The Mishnah (Hebrew: משנה) is the basic compilation of the Oral law of Judaism; according to the tradition, it was compiled in 189 CE. [74]

The source did not use the word "synagogue" explicitly, preferring the term basilica, a colonnaded building serving as a community center and commercial center. R. Judah, however, emphasized that the building was like a basilica; not an actual basilica.

The Tosefta clarified that building held religious ceremonies; not for casual gatherings.

It also mentioned a wooden platform as a focus for prayer and Torah readings. Most scholars have identified this building with what calls the greatest and most magnificent of the synagogues in the Alexandria. [75]

Conclusory Observations

The rhythms of the Jewish holidays from Rosh Hashana, Yom Kippur and Sukkot area continuation of the days of the Holy Temple. Rosh Hashana began the religious year. Yom Kippur was the Day of Atonement not only for individual but also communal sins. Sukkot was the fall festival of paramount importance in the agricultural society.

We also observed the importance of the shofar. Rosh Hashana was the festival of the shofar. Yom Kippur sounded the shofar at the end of the service, originally to announce the Jubilee Year the Rabbi's decided to sound the Shofar at the end of every Yom Kippur).

On Sukkot, the Jewish community petitioned God for a great harvest and future abundant rain to enable a hearty harvest.

The synagogue replaced the Holy Temple in lieu of the Sacrificial Cult. The Rabbi's kept the intent of Rosh Hashana and Yom Kippur. And they spiritualized the festival of Sukkot, Pesach and Shavuot, from petition for agricultural needs, to ones of remembrance and thanksgiving.

Interestingly, the shofar sounded during all the holidays in the Jewish year: The New Year, the Day of Atonement and the three-pilgrimage festival. For the three pilgrimage festivals there are three very different rituals that the Priests practiced in the Holy Temple.

Appendix A Biblical Sources for Praying for Jerusalem

Isa 45:3...........Father, You are the God of Israel, and they are Your people.

Isa 45:4...........You named them, though they did not know You.

Jer 33:8............Lord, cleanse them from their iniquities, and pardon all their sins.

Isa 45:17..........save them with an everlasting salvation.

Isa 45:13..........raise them up in righteousness and direct all their ways.

Ps 25:22..........redeem Israel out of all their troubles.

Joel 3:16..........be a shelter for Your people,

Joel 3:16..........and the strength of the children of Israel.

Jer 33:9............bring health and healing to them and to their land,

Jer 33:6............revealing to them Your abundance of peace and truth.

Jer 33:9............let Israel be to You a name of praise

Jer 33:9............and an honor before all the nations of the earth.

Jer 33:9............proclaiming all the good You do for them,

Jer 33:9............and causing fear and trembling among the nations,

Jer 33:9............because of the goodness and prosperity You provide.

Joel 2:25...........Restore everything that has been removed from them.

Joel 2:19...........Send them grain and new wine and oil to satisfy them.

Prov 16:7...........Make their enemies to be at peace with them

Joel 2:19............and no longer let them be a reproach among
the nations.

Eze 34:12..........Seek out Your sheep and deliver them

Eze 34:13..........from the peoples and countries where
scattered,

Eze 34:13..........and bring them to their own land.

Ps 122:6............I pray for the peace of Jerusalem,

Ps 122:6............may they prosper that love you.

Eze 34:25..........Lord, cause their enemies to cease from the
land.

Eze 34:26..........bless them and the places all around
Jerusalem.

Eze 34:26..........cause blessings to come down in their season.

Eze 34:27..........met Your people dwell safely in their land,

Jer 34:17...........delivered from trouble from all the kingdoms of
the earth.

Figure 26 Setting Fire to Jerusalem

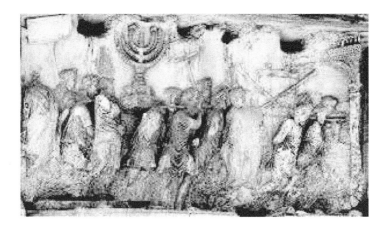

Figure 27 Jewish Captives and Temple Artifacts - Titus Arch

Figure 28 Lone Reminder of Temple Complex, Western Wall

Figure 29 Choshen, representing Israel's 12-tribes, worn by High Priest

Bibliography

Ben-Sasson, H.H. A History of the Jewish People, Harvard University Press, 1976,

Berkovitz, Jay R. *The Shaping of Jewish Identity in Nineteenth Century France.* Detroit, 1989.

Bonfil, Robert. *Jewish Life in Renaissance Italy.* Translated by Anthony Oldcorn. Berkeley, Calif., 1994.

Bright John, A History of Israel (Louisville, KY: Westminister Knox Press, 2000).

S. Brisman, History and Guide to Judaic Bibliography (1977).

Cohen, Richard I. *Jewish Icons: Art and Society in Modern Europe.* Berkeley, Calif., 1998.

Cohen, Shaye The beginnings of Jewishness (Berkeley and LA, CA: University of California Press, 1999).

Domnitch, Larry, "Western Wall: This remnant of the Second Temple is an important symbol in Judaism". yJewishLearning.com. Retrieved 15 March 2014.

Donin, , Hayim Halevy. To Be a Jew: A Guide to Jewish Observance in Contemporary Life. Basic guide to Jewish observance and practice from a very traditional point of view, (NY: Basic Books, 1972).

Dubin, Lois C. *The Port Jews of Habsburg Trieste: Absolutist Politics and Enlightenment Culture.* Stanford, Calif., 1999.

Ronald L. Eisenberg, The JPS Guide to Jewish Traditions: A JPS Desk Reference (Philadelphia: Jewish Publication Society, 2004

Endelman, Todd M. *The Jews of Georgian England, 1714–1830: Tradition and Change in a Liberal Society.* Philadelphia, 1979.

Frankel, Jonathan, and Steven J. Zipperstein, eds. *Assimilation and Community: The Jews in Nineteenth-Century Europe.* New York, 1991.

C. D. Ginsburg, Introduction to the Hebrew Bible, pp. 241 et seq., London, 1897

Gries, Ze'ev. *Conduct Literature: Its History and Place in the Life of Beshtian Hasidism* [in Hebrew]. Jerusalem, 1989.

Grayzel, Solomon, A History of the Jews, Penguin Books, 1984,

Horowitz, Elliott. "Coffee, Coffeehouses, and the Nocturnal Rituals of Early Modern Jewry." *Association for Jewish Studies Review* 14 (1989): 17–46.

Horowitz, Elliott. "The Eve of Circumcision: A Chapter in the History of Jewish Nightlife." *Journal of Social History* 23 (1989): 45–69.

Hyman, Paula E. *The Emancipation of the Jews of Alsace: Acculturation and Tradition in the Nineteenth Century.* New Haven, Conn., 1991.

Hyman, Paula E. *Gender and Assimilation in Modern Jewish History: The Roles and Representation of Women.* Seattle, Wash., 1995.

Idel, Moshe. *Kabbalah: New Perspectives.* New Haven, Conn., 1988.

Israel, Jonathan I. *European Jewry in the Age of Mercantilism, 1550–1750.* 3d ed. London, 1998.

Kaplan, Marion A. *The Making of the Jewish Middle Class: Women, Family, and Identity in Imperial Germany (*New York, 1991).

Katz, Jacob. *Divine Law in Human Hands: Study in Halakhic Flexibility.* Jerusalem, 1998.

Katz, Jacob. *Tradition and Crisis: Jewish Society at the End of the Middle Ages.* Translated by Bernard Dor Cooperman. New York, 1993.

Kauffman, Yehezkal, The Religion of Israel: From Its Beginning to the Babylonian Exile, Transl: Moshe Greenberg (Chicago: University of Chicago Press, 1960)

Kieval, Hillel J. *The Making of Czech Jewry.* New York, 1988.

Lowenstein, Steven M. *The Berlin Jewish Community: Enlightenment, Family, and Crisis, 1770–1830.* New York, 1994.

RaMBaM or Maimonides, Maimonides' Introduction to the Mishnah Torah: THE Complete Restatement Of The Oral Law (Mishneh Torah) (Jerusalem, Israel. Mechon Mamre, 2000)

Mendes-Flohr, Paul, and Reinharz, Jehuda. *The Jew in the Modern World.* 2d ed. New York, 1995.

Meyer, Michael A. *Response to Modernity: A History of the Reform Movement in Judaism.* New York, 1988.

Jacob Neusner 1984 Torah from our Sages (NY: Rossell Books. p. 175

Noth Martin, The History of Israel 1958). *History of Israel: Biblical History.* London: Adam & Charles Black

Pirkei Avot 5.21: "five for the Torah, ten for Mishnah, thirteen for the commandments, fifteen for Talmud".

The Jewish Contribution to Civilization (New York 1941)

Rozenblit, Marsha J. *The Jews of Vienna, 1867—1914: Assimilation and Identity.* Albany, N.Y., 1983.

Ruderman, David. *Jewish Thought and Scientific Discovery in Early Modern Europe.* New Haven, Conn., 1995.

Scholem, Gershom. *Major Trends in Jewish Mysticism.* 3d rev. ed. New York, 1954.

Shulvass, Moses A. *From East to West*. Detroit, 1971.

Strack, Hermann, Introduction to the Talmud and Midrash, Jewish Publication Society, 1945. pp. 11–12. "[The Oral Law] was handed down by word of mouth during a long period.

Tirosh-Rothschild, Hava. "Jewish Culture in Renaissance Italy: A Methodological Survey." *Italia* 9 (1990): 63–96.

Isaac Unterman,The Jewish Holidays (New York: Bloch Publishing Co., 1950 (2nd edition)

Urbach, Ephraim, The Sages (Jerusalem: Varda Books. 2006).

Zipperstein, Steven J. *The Jews of Odessa: A Cultural History, 1794–1881*. Stanford, Calif., 1985.

Endnotes

---

1 The Jewish way in Death and Mourning, Maurice Lamm, New York: Jonathan

David Publishers, 2000 (also available online at www.chabad.org/)

2 Prov 3:19-20

3 Joshua Berman, The Temple: Its Symbolism and Meaning, Then and Now (Northvale, NJ: Jason Aronson, Inc., 1995)

4 Joshua Berman, The Temple: Its Symbolism and Meaning, Then and Now (Northvale, NJ: Jason Aronson, 1995).

5 Ner Tamid, https://www.jewishvirtuallibrary.org/ner-tamid

6 Fried, Lisbeth S. (2014). Ezra and the Law in History and Tradition. Univ of South Carolina Press.

7 2 Kings 17; Josephus, Antiquities 9.277–91

8 Fried, Lisbeth S. (2014). Ezra and the Law in History and Tradition. Univ of South Carolina Press.

9 Samaritans. https://en.m.wikipedia.org/wiki/Samaritans - cite_note-10

10 Fried, Lisbeth S. (2014). Ezra and the Law in History and Tradition. Univ of South Carolina Press.

11 Clarke's Commentary on the Bible - 2 Kings 17:30

12 Fried, Lisbeth S. (2014). Ezra and the Law in History and Tradition. Univ of South Carolina Press.

13 Barbati, Gabrielle (January 21, 2013). "Israeli Election Preview: The Samaritans, Caught Between Two Votes". International Business Times. Retrieved 14 October 2014.

14 Josephus 1.14.

15 E. Baneth, On the origin of the Sadducees and the Boethusians, , Dessau, DE, 1882);

16 Siobhan F. N. Marshall, A Study of Boethian Metaphysics, Dist., (New York: Fordham University, 1998).

17 (Shabbat. 108a; Soferim i. 2);

18 The Oxford Dictionary of the Jewish Religion - Adele Berlin, Maxine L. Grossman - 2011 - Page 148 "The rabbis considered them primarily a religious sect, founded by Boethus, a heretical disciple of the Mishnaic authority ... Other scholars connect the Boethusians with Shimon ben Boethus, high priest in King Herod's time; the family is "

19 Sadducees, https://www.livius.org/articles/people/sadducees/, Accessed 27 April 2019.

20 Eusebius of Caesarea in Praeparatio Evangelica, Book VIII, chapter 11.

21 Josephus, Antiquities, 15.10.4 [371,2].

22 Pliny, Natural History, V, 17,4.

23 Ravit Rotberg-Ferber, Qumeran Sectarians and Jewish Law, Law, Dist. (London: London University , 1978).

24 Frank Moore Cross, Jr., The Ancient Library of Qumran and Modern Biblical Studies (Garden City, NY: Anchor Books, 1958), p. 51. Another view of the derivation is to relate the word to Hebrew 'esa, "council,"--the party of the council (Andre Dupont-Sommer, The Essene Writings of Qumran, p. 43).

25 See J. T. Milik, Ten Years of Discovery in the Wilderness of Judaea (London: SCM Press, 1959), p. 80, n. 1. The original discovery was made by Cantineau and written up in Syria 14 (1933):177.

26 James Strong, Lexicon

27 Teppler, Yaakov Y; Weingarten, Susan (2007), Birkat haMinim: Jews and Christians in conflict in the ancient world,

28 Pliney, Essenes.12 Josephus, Wars, 2.8.5 [124]; Philo, Apologia, 1

29 Josephus, Wars, 2.8.10 [150].

30 Pliny, V.17.4; Philo, Apologia, 11; Quod omnis, 77; Josephus, Wars, 2.8.3 [122].

31 Philo, Apologia, 14-17

32 Josephus, Wars, 2.8.2 [121] and 8.13 [160].

33 Josephus, Wars, 2.8.11 [157].

34 Philo, Quod omnis, 76; Josephus, Wars, 2.8.5 [128-133].

35 Philo, Quod omnis, 81,82; Josephus, Antiquities, 18.1.5; Josephus, Wars, 2.8.3.

36 Josephus, Wars, 2.8.8.

37 Philo, Quod omnis, 87, and Apologia, 13.

38 Josephus, Wars, 2.8.10.

39 Jeffrey Harrison Nazarene Christianity: John Toland on the Early Church, Thesis (Long Beach:California State University, 2001).

40 Heschel, Susannah, Abraham Geiger on the origins of Christianity, Dist., (Philadelphia, PA: University of Pennsylvania, 1989)

41 Panarion 29.3.3; Margolis and Marx, pp. 199-200

42 David C. Sim The Gospel of Matthew and Christian Judaism 1998 p182 "The Nazarenes are first mentioned by Epiphanius who records that they upheld the Torah, including the practice of circumcision and sabbath observance (Panarion 29:5.4; 7:2, 5; 8:1-7),

43 Jonathan Bourgel, "The Jewish Christians' Move from Jerusalem as a pragmatic choice", in: Dan Jaffe (ed), Studies in Rabbinic Judaism and Early Christianity, Leyden: Brill, 2010}; . Blunt, John Henry, Dictionary of Sects, Heresies, Ecclesiastical Parties and Schools of Religious Thought. (London, Oxford and Cambridge: Rivingtons, 1874).

44 Gregory Spinner, After the Temple, Before The World: Redefining Sacrifice In Ancient And Medieval Judaism, Dist., (Chicago: University of Chicago, 2003).

45 Ronald L. Eisenberg, The JPS Guide to Jewish Traditions: A JPS Desk Reference (Philadelphia: Jewish Publication Society, 2004

46 Mishnah Pesachim 64

47 Mishnah Pesachim 64

48 . Donin, Hayim H. To Pray as a Jew: A Guide To The Prayer Book and The Synagogue Service. (New York: Basic Books. 1991).

49 Hayim H. Donin (10 October 1991). To pray as a Jew: a guide to the prayer book and the synagogue service. Basic Books

50 Seder Conclusion. https://www.aish.com/h/pes/h/Seder-Conclusion.html

51 Seder Conclusion, https://www.aish.com/h/pes/h/Seder-Conclusion.html

52 Special Sabbaths, https://www.jewishvirtuallibrary.org/special-shabbats

53 Donin, , Hayim Halevy. To Be a Jew: A Guide to Jewish Observance in Contemporary Life. Basic guide to Jewish observance and practice from a very traditional point of view, (NY: Basic Books, 1972).

54 Chatam Sofer, Yoreh De'ah 332.

55 See Alfred Edersheim, History of the Jewish Nation after the Destruction of Jerusalem by Titus (Edinburgh, 1856).

56 Morse, Steve. "Jewish Calendar Rules". stevemorse.org. Retrieved 14 March 2019.

57 Rabbi Dr. Reuven Hammer Entering the High Holy Days. Reprinted with permission from the Jewish Publication Society; Alfred Edersheim, The Temple: Its Ministry and Services, The New Moons: The Feast of the Seventh New Moon, or of Trumpets, or New Year's Day; Morse, Steve. "Jewish Calendar Rules". stevemorse.org. Retrieved 14 March 2019. .

58 Num. 10:1 ff.; 1 Chron. 15: 24.

59 "Musical Instruments," Interpreter's Dictionary of the Bible, p. 472; Arthur L. Finkle.;Easy Guide to Shofar Sounding, LA: Torah Aura, 2002; Sidney B. Hoenig, Origins of the Rosh Hashanah Liturgy, The Jewish Quarterly Review, New Series, Vol. 57, The Seventy-Fifth Anniversary Volume of the Jewish Quarterly Review (1967), pp. 312-331, University of Pennsylvania Press; JPS Torah Commentary – Leviticus, Commentary Baruch A. Levine, Philadelphia: JPS, 1989; David Wulstan, The Sounding of the Shofar Author(s): Source: The Galpin Society Journal, Vol. 26 (May, 1973), pp. 29-46,Galpin Society; Solomon Zeitlin, An Historical Study of the First Canonization of the Hebrew Liturgy, The Jewish Quarterly Review, New Series, Vol. 36, No. 3 (Jan., 1946), pp. 211-229, University of Pennsylvania Press

60 Mishneh Berurah 590:2

61 Tractate Yoma, Ch. 1-8.

62 See Rabbi Dr. Reuven Hammer, Entering the High Holy Days. Reprinted with permission from the Jewish Publication Society, 1998.

[63] Fasting And Fast Days. https://www.jewishvirtuallibrary.org/fasting-and-fast-days

[64] Fasting and Fast Days. https://www.jewishvirtuallibrary.org/fasting-and-fast-days

65 David Mescheloff, How Dd Judaism Recover from the Loss of the Temple in Jerusalem. https://www.quora.com/How-did-Judaism-recover-from-the-loss-of-the-Temple-in-Jerusalem

66 Shaye J. D. Cohen, "The Temple and the Synagogue," in The Temple in Antiquity: Ancient Records and Modern Perspectives, ed. Truman G. Madsen (Provo, UT: Religious Studies Center, Brigham Young University, 1984)

67 Chad Spigel, "First Century Synagogues", n.p. [cited 21 Jul 2019]. Online: https://www.bibleodyssey.org:443/en/places/related-articles/first-century-synagogues

---

68 Kohanim Forever: From the Sources. http://www.cohen-levi.org/the_tribe/kohanim_forever.htm

God's promise to Aaron and his sons of continuity throughout all generations is mentioned repeatedly in the Written Torah, the Prophets and the Oral Torah.

Torah: "Bring close Aaron your brother and his sons with him from among the children of Israel to become Kohanim/Priests to Me." (Exodus 28:1) (Every use of the Hebrew word Li, "to me" is for all time—Midrash Gadol)

"and they shall have the Kehuna/Priesthood as a statute forever, and you shall consecrate Aaron and his sons." (Exodus 29:9); "And anoint them as you anointed their father, that they may serve Me, and it shall be for them an appointment to an everlasting Kehuna/Priesthood throughout their generations." (Exodus 40:15); "You and your sons with you shall keep your Kehuna/Priesthood, I give your Kehuna/Priesthood as a gift of service." (Numbers 18:17); "It is an everlasting covenant of salt before God with you and with your descendants." (Numbers 18: 19); "And it shall be to him and to his descendants after him a covenant of everlasting Kehuna/Priesthood." (Numbers 25:13); "For God your God has chosen him of all your tribes to stand and serve with the name of God he and his sons forever." (Deuteronomy 18:5).

Also see Ezekiel 44:15; Malachi 2:7; Mishna Middos 5:4; Gemara Kiddushin 71a, etc..

69 Rachel Hachlili , Ancient Synagogues—Archaeology and Art (Brill, 2013); Dr. David Gurevich, Magdala's Stone of Contention. https://bibleinterp.arizona.edu/articles/magdalas-stone-contention

70 See U. Kaploun, ed., The Synagogue (1973); A. Eisenberg, The Synagogue through the Ages (1974); C. H. Krinsky,Synagogues of Europe (1987); Beit Trfillah.

https://encyclopedia2.thefreedictionary.com/Beit+Tefillah

71 History of the Bible.

http://www.historyworld.net/wrldhis/PlainTextHistories.asp?ParagraphID=a
db1

72 Chad Spigel, "First Century Synagogues Online:

https://www.bibleodyssey.org:443/en/places/related-articles/first-century-
synagogues

73 Chad Spigel, Ancient Synagogue Seating Capacities: Methodology,
Analysis and Limits. (Tübingen, Germany.: Mohr Siebeck, 2012

74 The Tosefta corresponded to the Mishnah, with the same divisions and
tractates; M. Aberbach, Labor, Crafts and Commerce in Ancient Israel
(Jerusalem, 1994)

75 Philo, in Legatio ad Caium; Lieberman, Tosefta Ki-Fshutah, Mo'ed, (New
York, 1962); E. Schiirer, The History of the Jewish People in the Time of
Jesus Christ, rev. and ed. G. Vermes and E Millar (Edinburgh, 1979); Kasher,
The Jews in Hellenistic and Roman Egypt (Tiubingen, 1985); The Ancient
Synagogue as an Economic Center Author(s): Ben-Zion Rosenfeld and
Joseph Menirav,, Journal of Near Eastern Studies, Vol. 58, No. 4 (Oct.,
1999), pp. 259-276 Published by: The University of Chicago Press Stable
URL: https://www.jstor.org/stable/546161 Accessed: 31-07-2019 15:06
UTC.

Made in the USA
Monee, IL
09 January 2021